How May I Serve You?
José García Oliva

Content

Preface	p. 06
Abstract	08
Introduction	10
Diagram	22
Live-chat transcripts	24
Chat index (Saadia)	25
Chat index (Malik)	71
Way forward	110
Biography	112
References	113
Acknowledgement	114
Colophon	115

fig.			
	01	*We Use English Names 1/2*	p. 2,3
	02	*Customer services (screenshots)*	6,7
	03	*HMISU website 1/2*	12
	04	*HMISU website 2/2*	13
	05	*Agents and cubicles*	16
	06	*Headset*	16
	07	*Night shift*	16
	08	*Hands and mouse*	17
	09	*Blue light*	17
	10	*Empty cubicles*	17
	11	*Mind map*	22,23
	12	*I Like To Use My Real Name*	30
	13	*Framed a*	31
	14	*Install shot (screen)*	42,43
	15	*Keep on Smiling*	44
	16	*Install shot (frames)*	54,55
	17	*Install shot (stools)*	55
	18	*But I Still Have a Job*	56
	19	*Framed b*	57
	20	*Install shot (cubicles)*	80
	21	*Install shot (computer)*	80,81
	22	*Audience 01*	82
	23	*Audience 02*	82
	24	*Audience 03*	82
	25	*Audience 04*	83
	26	*Audience 05*	83
	27	*Audience 06*	83
	28	*Screen divider (photos) 1/2*	84
	29	*Screen divider (mirror)*	84,85
	30	*Screen divider (photos) 2/2*	85
	31	*Well Behaved*	102
	32	*Framed c*	103
	33	*Untitled (perfect lovers) 1/2*	106
	34	*Website (PKT-GMT time zone)*	106
	35	*Untitled (perfect lovers) 2/2*	107
	36	*We Use English Names 2/2*	117

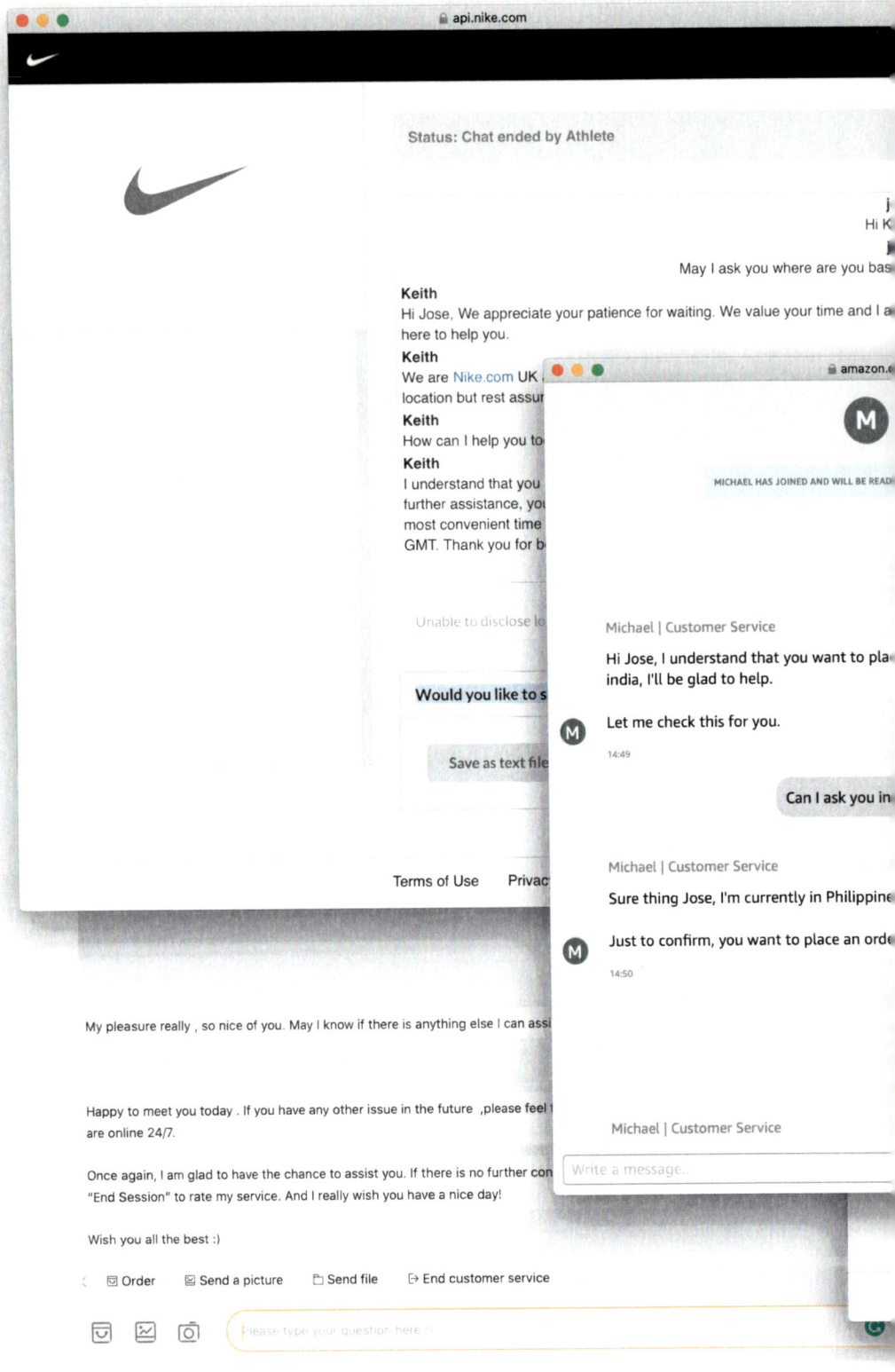

PREFACE

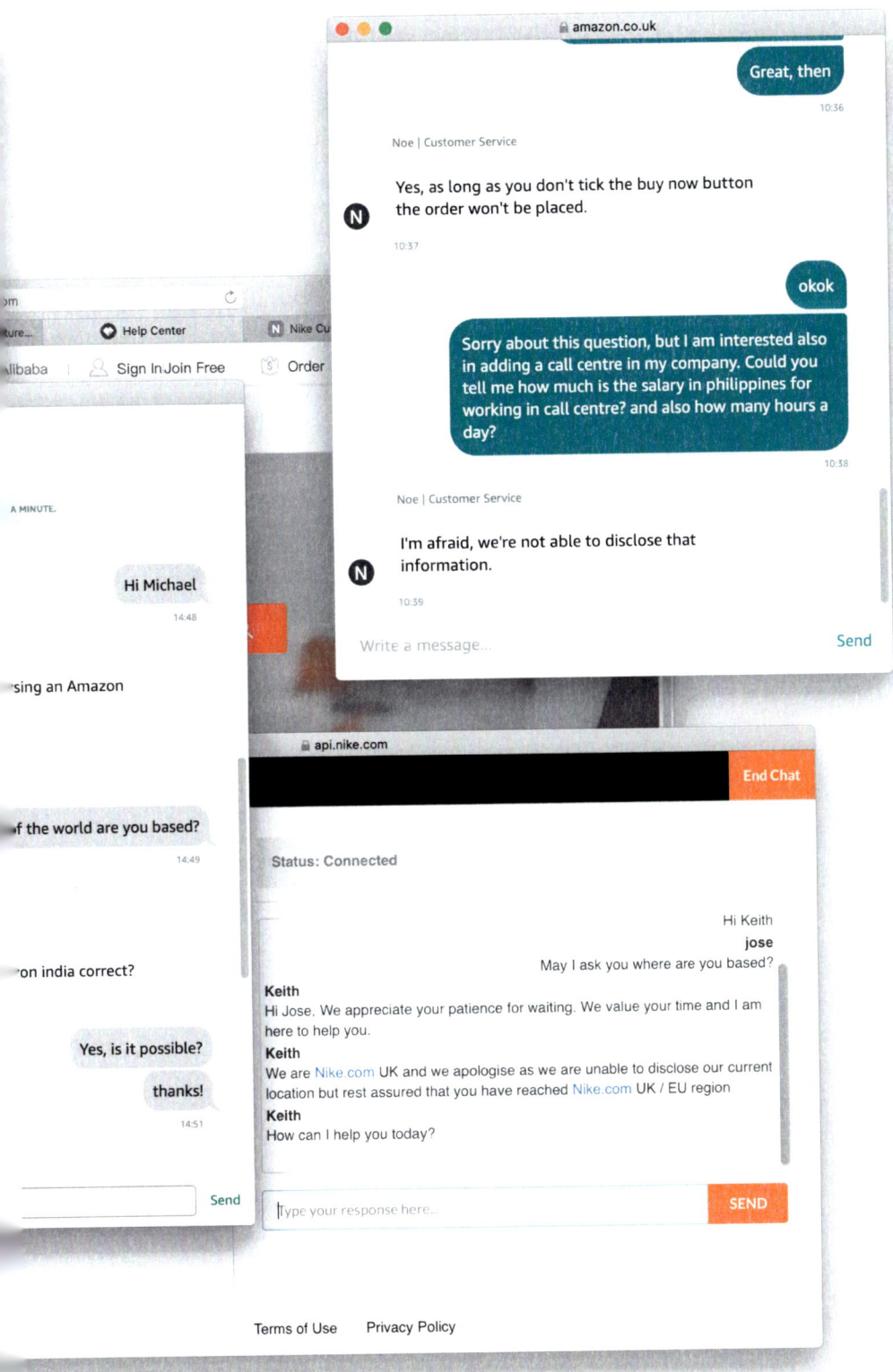

How May I Serve You?
José García Oliva

The hidden workers providing offshore outsourced online customer services are still suffering from the significant consequences of colonial systems. This report is based on a review of 158 live-chat conversations between members of an online audience and two customer service agents based in Pakistan and outsourced by UK companies.

This online chat platform was created and designed for the participatory art project 'How May I Serve You?''. Analysis of the conversations demonstrated how outsourced companies survey eployees' chats and physical behaviour, threaten pay cuts or dismissal, and demand that agents lie about their identity. Further research is needed to identify practical solutions to improve employees' working conditions in the online customer service industry.

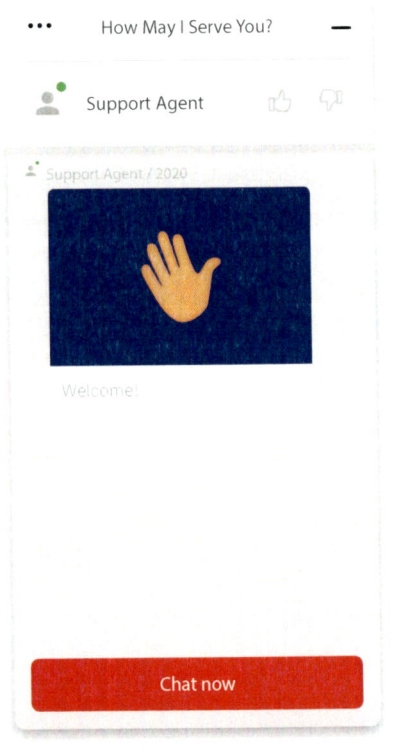

Call centre /
Offshore outsourcing /
Participatory art /
Live-chat /
Online identity /
Low-Cost Countries Sourcing /
Labour /
Bridging art /

As a result of the Covid-19 pandemic, for some, who are working from home and physically isolated, the main and only open window is the internet. This heterotopic site, germinated in the 1990s, currently hosts an e-public space for human interactions, namely, a sphere for global connectivity. Even though it cannot yet replicate social encounters, it has enabled us to work collectively at both a national and an international scale. Now, when everything feels virtually interconnected, on the other side of the screen the theatre of globalisation is growing, continuing to pixelate the poorer communities working in Low-Cost Countries Sourcing (LCCS).

These outsourced elements are one of the main engines facilitating the neoliberalist system, enabling corporations to continue to generate products and services with the lowest possible expenditure. Within this give-and-take scheme emerges a global hierarchical model where one part of the system exploits and the other is exploited (which is nothing new in human history). For example, on the back of Apple devices is written: 'Designed by Apple in California. Assembled in China/India/Vietnam'. But where in China? In which city in India? Which Vietnamese province? These phrases exemplify what outsourcing is about, from power structure to invisible cities, invisible labour and hidden people.

Another example of outsourcing — and the one in which I will explore further here — is online customer service platforms. When you have a complaint about your slow wi-fi speed and immediately contact the broadband online help centre to ask: 'My internet has been slow for two hours, what's going on?', before you've finished typing, you've received an automated message that says: 'We are very sorry, but all our agents are engaged right now. If you can hold for a few minutes, we'll reach out to you as soon as possible'. While you are waiting in front of your computer, someone on the other side of the world, is putting their headset on, ready to help you solve your problem, at the same time helping three or four other people. This simulation is an 'online customer service platform'.

Perhaps it is a coincidence that some of the countries providing these services have been previously colonised by the countries which require them. Spain, for instance, has many call centres working for national companies in different countries in South America. The United Kingdom also parallels this relationship between customer/service – coloniser/colonised. Pakistan is one of the leading countries that the United Kingdom outsources its call centres to, along, of course, with India. Among the reasons for this are their fluent English (another effect of colonialism) and the availability of low-cost labour. This current political and economic position in both countries creates a rigid power system where one monopolises and the other serves.

Whilst I am discussing these issues I will delve into the art project I started in 2019, titled 'How May I Serve You'[1]. The aim of this project was to shed some sobering light on the current structure of this labour. This online site-specific platform was made in collaboration with two current call centre agents from, and based in, Islamabad, Pakistan, Malik Ayaz and

Since the start of the project, three online performances have taken place. The first occurred in July 2020, funded by the Royal College of Art and the second in September 2021, commissioned and exhibited at The World Transformed festival. The third performance happened in November 2022 and was commissioned by Axisweb and funded by Arts Council England. This time, in parallel, a physical exhibition was shown at SET Kensington, which consisted of a recreation of four cubicle desks and a series of pieces that materialised some of the quotes from the previous live-chat conversations. Between the three performances, a total of 346 people joined the chat and started a conversation.

1 The total amount of the funds for the first and second online performances went to both Malik and Saadia for their time, participation and collaboration to make 'How May I Serve You' materialised. The third time, 50% of the funds went to them, and the other half covered the expenses of the recreation of the cubicle desks and installation of the physical exhibition. Calculated per hour, the fee paid to Malik and Saadia was £38 an hour.

Saadia Abbasi, who are outsourced by UK companies –The site has a biographical description of each and the comparative time zones of Pakistan and the United Kingdom. The platform replicates the aesthetics of a live-chat service where people have the opportunity to interact through open conversations – one at a time – with either one of them. The project aims to connect the customer to the agents in a completely different setting; there is no commodity involved, but a space to facilitate this exchange, to ignite dialogues and ultimately to archive these conversations that reveal our current system of socio-economic and political oppression. As Oliver Marchart says in his book Conflictual Aesthetics: 'A political situation cannot simply be constructed, it must also be encountered' (2019: 38). Thus, public participation is needed.

'How May I Serve You' first took place on 24 July 2020 during the Royal College of Art online MA Degree Show. The event lasted for eight hours, during which time Malik and Saadia would either pose a question or answer anything they wanted to talk about with the people joining the platform. During this time 158 people joined the chat and a variety of topics were discussed.

Malik, with a Master's in Management, has worked in customer service for sixteen years. Saadia, with a postgraduate qualification in Sociology, is currently working as a customer service representative in an outsourced call centre. Both Malik and Saadia are providing services to clients based in the United States and United Kingdom.

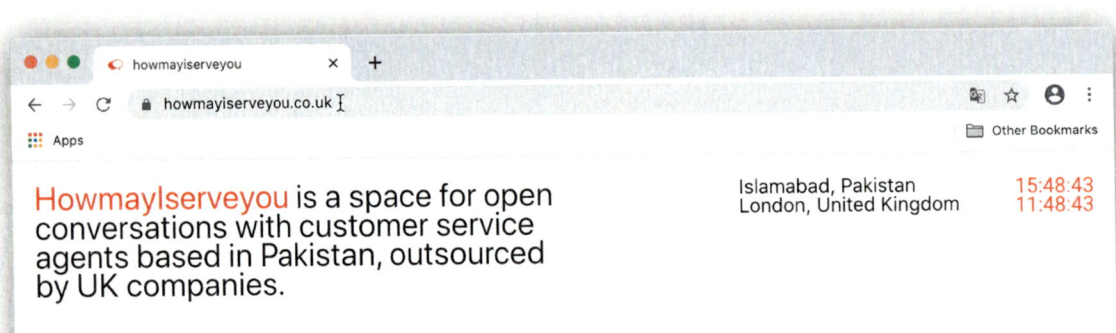

Howmaylserveyou is a space for open conversations with customer service agents based in Pakistan, outsourced by UK companies.

Islamabad, Pakistan   15:48:43
London, United Kingdom 11:48:43

Timetable

Chat with Saadia
PKT 14.00 — 18.00
GMT 10.00 — 14.00

Chat with Ayaz
PKT 20.00 — 00.00
GMT 16.00 — 20.00

Saadia Abbasi started her career as a Customer Service Representative from a Pakistani telecom company, called Jazz. She currently has 8 years of diversified experience within the Call Centre industry. She has also been working for HRSG and Ibex group in the same capacity. At the present time, she is working in a call centre named Next-Gen, based in Pakistan, which provides customer service to both the United Kingdom and the United States of America based clients. She was born in Rawalpindi, Pakistan and holds a Masters in Sociology degree.

Malik Ayaz has worked in a call centre for 16 years, starting from an agent back in 2005 from Pakistan's leading telecom (Jazz). He has worked almost in all domains of call centre including inbound, outbound, quality assurance, front end and back end operation. He has worked with European companies as a consultant to start their call centres in Pakistan and to establish call centres in Kenya and Myanmar. His recent assignment was Head of Call Centre Operations for Brighterlite. He is from Islamabad, Pakistan. He is an MBA and a computer science graduate.

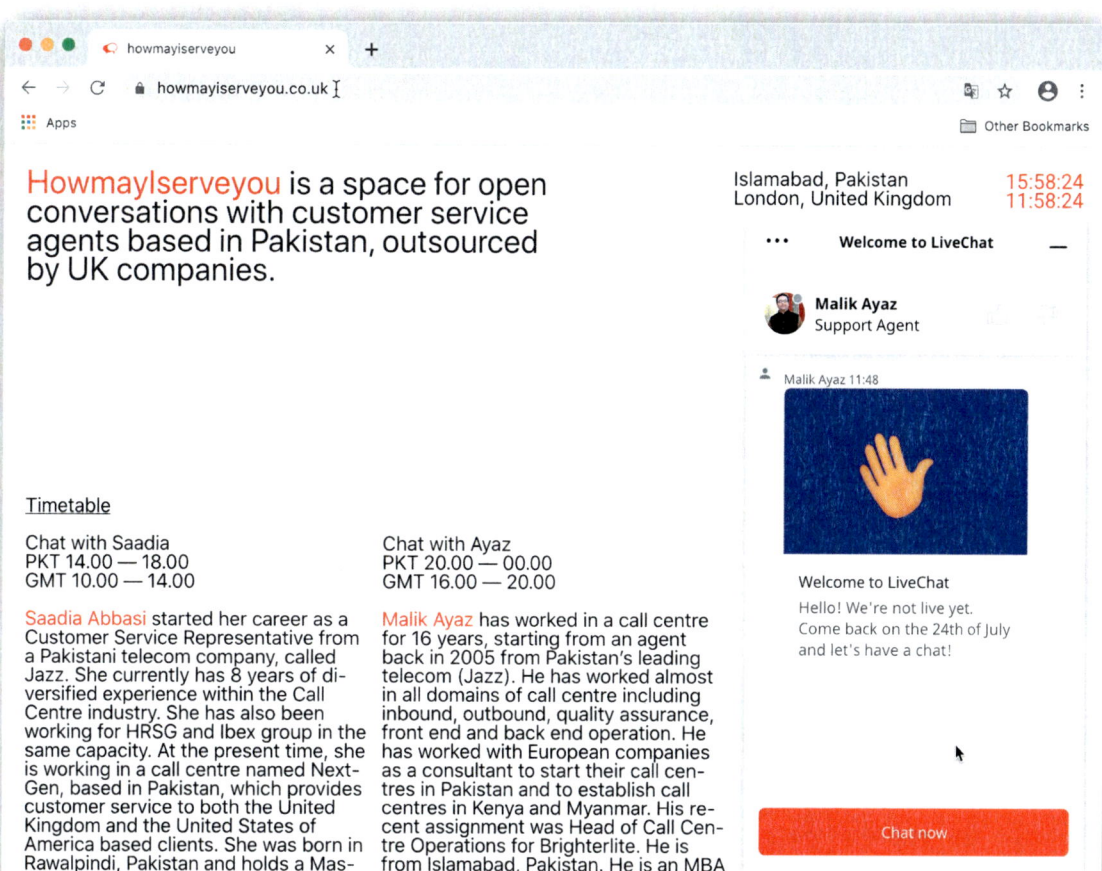

03 How May I Serve You? (Ask us anything!)
    2020, Website, Full page screen capture.
04 How May I Serve You? (Welcome to LiveChat)
    2020, website. Full page screen capture.

INTRODUCTION   13

In this artwork, the visitor becomes a user of the platform, the website becomes the exhibition space and the chat is the outcome. The project goes beyond spectatorship, as it intends to give real agency to both participants — the customer and the agent. Conversations are two-way streams in which the personal and public can meet and mingle.

In these live-chat conversations, the active spectators and the agents have the opportunity to decide by themselves which questions they want to ask or to answer, and this format alone enriches and elaborates the dialogues. It is important that a conversation is maintained between the actors, as this creates spontaneity, and overrides the somewhat 'interview-like' arrangement that we have come to know in online chat scenarios.

Through reading the transcript of all these conversations, some themes come up repeatedly; for example, the call centre structure, labour and identity, and many questions regarding automation.

When I think of call centres, what comes to my mind is Lars Tunbjörk's Office series of photographs: everyone wearing headsets, 'sterile walls, dust-free desks and well-vacuumed cubicles' (Kors 2012). Between rows of cubicles, one beside the other, a supervisor is observing every action each agent is performing — reflecting the repeated warning in George Orwell's novel Nineteen Eighty-Four, 'Big Brother is watching you' (Orwell [1949] 2008: 3). This is why these spaces are referred to as 'electronic panopticons' (Bain and Taylor 2020: 2). The conversations between Malik and a participant demonstrate how a call centre operates:

London, United Kingdom
Customer

Islamabad, Pakistan
Malik Ayaz

> My question is: what is the physical architecture of a call centre?
>
> Are you all in one big room?
>
> What environment you live in?
>
> 18.12 GMT

16,17   fig. 05,08,10

> We all sit in a big hall, with sound proofing on walls and have our own cubicles
>
> When one agent finishes his shift then the other can utilize that particular cubicle
>
> 23.13 PKT

> Do you see each other or the cubicles are solid surfaces?
>
> 18.15 GMT

16,17   fig. 05,10

> They are solid surfaces, these are made of wood. In few call centres we have mirrors in place right in front of us so that we can see our facial expressions while talking to customers and keep ourselves smiling all the times.
>
> 23.18 PKT

These mirror devices that work as reminders for maintaining certain behaviours are one of the features of working in customer services. The idea of being polite and controlling your emotions is something that you must master in order not to be either fired or take a pay cut. These conditions are psychologically draining, as Saadia explained here in one of the conversations during the live chat:

We are being treated as machines and not humans. We are monitored all the time and that's not mentally healthy, but one has to earn. How would you feel if you chatted with 7/8 people at the same time [...] It's my job to smile even if I don't want to. We need to serve every cus-

Agents and cubicles, 2020 Captured by Malik Ayaz.   05
Headset, 2020 Captured by Malik Ayaz.   06
Night shift, 2020 Captured by Malik Ayaz.   07

08   *Mouse and Hands,* 2020 Captured by Malik Ayaz.
09   *Blue Light,* 2020 Captured by Malik Ayaz.
10   *Cubicles,* 2020 Captured by Malik Ayaz.

tomer with a smile on our face, and trust me I am chatting with you and I have that smile on my face, which you will see in any customer service centre and we are given training for maintaining this convivial behaviour. It is difficult though [...] as we are also humans and mood swings are always there, but we have strict quality checks on us and we need to give that feeling to the customer which makes him comfortable and makes him think that he is at the right place.

The mirror device is an intense confrontation, seeing yourself while you are smiling to the virtual Western customer. At the moment when we see our reflection we are also seeing an identity that represents us. In an online customer service setting, these identities need to be translated. In these cyberspaces, both our body and its physical relationship to a place evaporate. Afterwards, what happens is that your identity transforms into a profile. Translations can be manipulated for the benefits of the translator, in this case the corporation. To exemplify this mutational process, Saadia explains it very well:

> Do you change your accent based on specific situations or context?
> 15.20 GMT

> Yes, we do change our accents as per analysing language, the needs of customer, and it is difficult for us too.
> 20.20 PKT

> Do you need to use different vocabulary when you talk to me, just to sound more British?
> 15.21 GMT

> ...

> Yes! We even watch movies, videos and are trained by professionals to use the right accent
>
> 20.22 PKT

How do you feel about that? About having the 'right' accent?

15.24 GMT

> It's really important, as a customer feels that he has found the right person to talk to
>
> 20.26 PKT

Why do you think that? Isn't someone from Pakistan with their own accent a 'right person?'

20.35 GMT

> I mean to say that a person thinks that he is talking to the right person like even if my name is Saadia, but while talking to a customer in UK I would use Anna and they feel better about it.
>
> But I personally feel that it's wrong
>
> I like to use my real name, but unfortunately to make a customer feel that he is talking to a real English guy, we need to use English names.
>
> I always feel bad about hiding my name, and why should I? If I am Saadia then I am Saadia and not Anna or Elsa or Nicky, etc.
>
> Companies should not fake things from the customers. But I have to do it, due to their policy restrictions.
>
> 20.39 PKT

So, they're basically obligating you to lie?

15.39 PKT

> Exactly!
>
> It feels extremely hypocritical when I tell my kids that lie is not acceptable, and then, I lie about my name everyday at work.
>
> 20.40 PKT

What Abbasi describes is the everyday reality; this is what happens on the other side of our screens when we engage with an online help centre. In these online interactions we are dealing with complaints but simultaneously we are unconsciously allowing outsourcing models to hide people's identities. We inadvertently strengthen the perpetuation of a policy which has racism embedded in its foundations. This phenomenon has an enormous effect on the socio-emotional well-being of people's lives.

The problems and solutions of these workers are there – as they say – but we need a combination of practices to solve it by direct action.

'How May I Serve You' is admittedly a symbolic action. But it does reveal that these practices are still taking place today. This project was developed to be a participatory performance where people have agency in their interactions, aiming to ignite engagement and bring about empathy through being actively present. It is important to note that the intention in this text is not to critique the use of outsourcing platforms, but to question the use of it as a channel that duplicates a colonial system and that dehumanises others for the sake of profit.

I like to see these forms of actions as bridges where conversations can cross from one place to another (from someone to someone else). Participation is what makes the bridge viable and sustainable, and if the bridge is crossable, then empathy is on the other side

The diagram on the next page shows all the different iterations of *How May I Serve You?*, including the website, the physical (ex)position and the book. This mind map is the bigger picture of the project and displays the interrelation in its multiple formats.

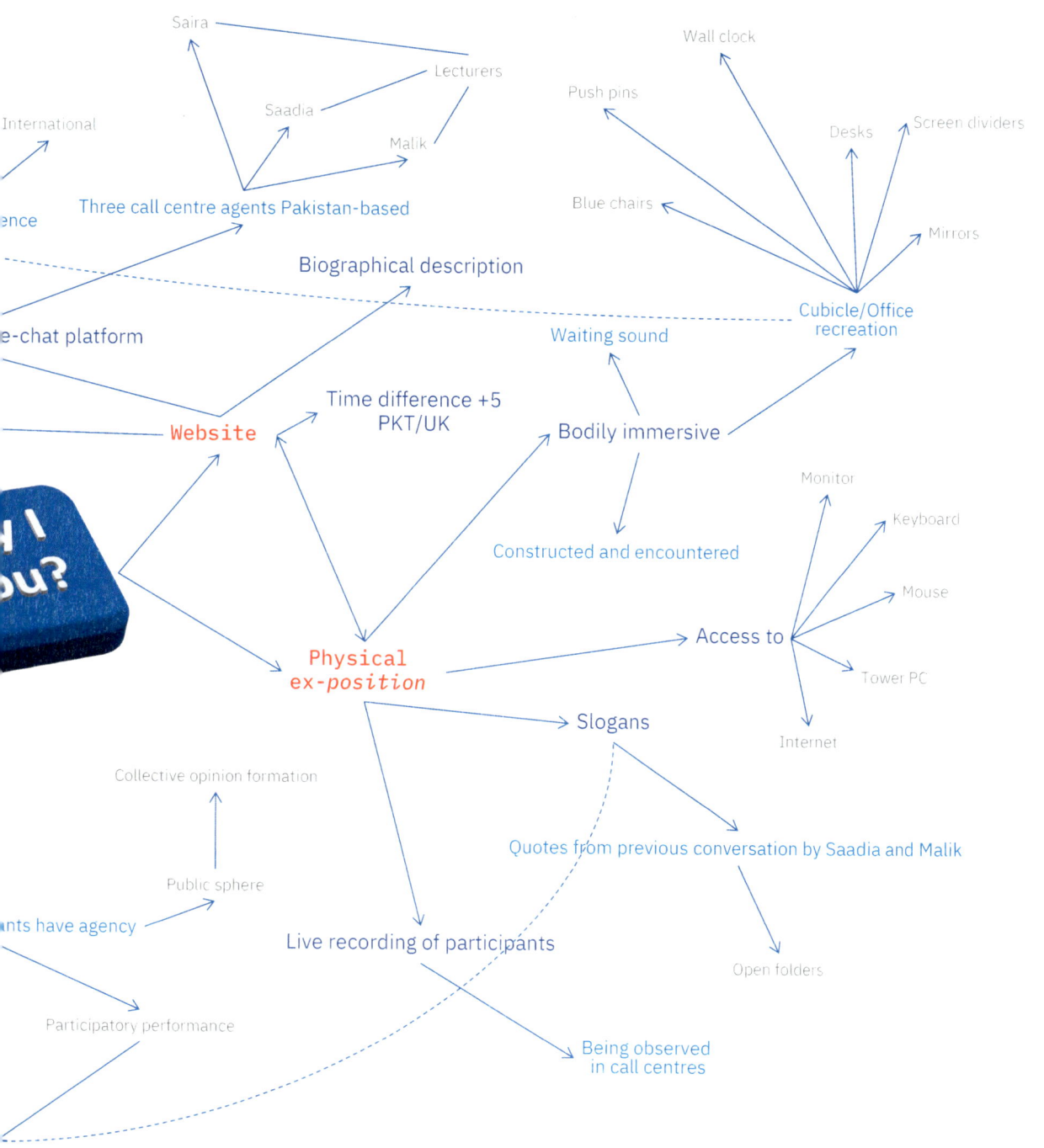

Live chat
Saadia Abbasi

Transcripts
José García Oliva

#

greetings (p.26) weather (26) accents (27) identity (28) colonialism (29)(32) migration (29)(32) globalisation (32) outsourcing (32)(49)(53) wage (33)(51) unions (34) jobinsecurity (34) workingconditions (36)(38)(39)(40)(58) automation (36)(41)(48) customers (40)(48)(61) script (46) family(50)(52)(63) genderhierarchy (58) herassment (60) livechatplatform (63) travel (65) love (65) religion (66) farewell (67)

fig.

12 *I Like To Use My Real Name*	p.30
13 *Framed a*	31
14 *Install shot a*	42,43
15 *Keep on Smiling*	44
16 *Install shot b*	54,55
17 *But I Still Have a Job*	56
18 *Framed b*	57

In the following pages, you will find a selection of the conversations between visitors and Saadia Abbasi. The chats have been shortened and connected from one discussion to another in order to keep continuity in the subject matter and improve the writing flow. The chat order hasn't changed, and all the words were kept the same, including colloquialism, acronyms and misspellings

London, United Kingdom
Customer

Islamabad, Pakistan
Saadia Abbasi

> Hello, how may I help you?
> 20.10 PKT

Hi, nice to meet you Saadia

how are you this morning?
15.11 GMT

> i am good
>
> how are you?
> 20.11 PKT

my dog is ill!
15.12 GMT

> how can i help you with that?
> 20.12 PKT

she is old. my dad took her to the vets today
15.13 BST

> Awww!!!!
>
> really sorry to read that
> 20.13 PKT

have you ever had a pet?
15.13 GMT

> Yeah i had a pair of cats
> 20.14 PKT

names?
15.14 GMT

> Elsa and Anna :)
> 20.15 PKT

nice

can I ask you about your job?
15.15 GMT

> Yes Please
> 20.15 PKT

How is Islamabad today?
15.15 GMT

> It's humid
>
> have you ever called a call centre?
> 20.16 PKT

Many times.
15.16 GMT

I get very frustrated dealing with some call services when I discover they are just 'going through the motion' and it seems to take for ever.

I will frequently try to escalate the conversation and aim to speak to someone higher up the ladder.

When I was in America I would frequently get comments on my accent.

Of course I wouldn't view the way I speak as having an accent.

I was also fascinated discovering how different accent play a role.

15.18 GMT

yes accent is very important

20.19 PKT

Do you change your accent based on specific situations or context?

15.20 GMT

Yes we do change our accents as per analysing language needs of customer and it is difficult for us too

20.20 PKT

Do you need to use different vocabulary when you talk by here, just to sound more British?

15.21 GMT

Yes! even we watch movies, videos and are trained by professionals to use the right assent

accent*

20.22 PKT

how do you feel about that? About having the "right accent"?

15.24 GMT

its really important as a customer feels that he has found the right person to talk to

20.26 PKT

Why do you think is that? Isn't someone from Pakistan with their own accent a 'right person'?

15.35 GMT

> i mean to say that a person thinks that he is talking to the right person
>
> like even if my name is Saadia, but while talking to a customer in the UK i would use Anna and they feel better about it
>
> but i personally feel that its wrong
>
> companies should not fake things from the customers
>
> 20.39 PKT

That's definitely wrong... completely unethical

So they're basically obligating you to lie?

15.39 GMT

> Exactly!
>
> we are not allowed to use our own names
>
> 20.40 PKT

I didn't know all that... it's shocking

do you use multiple names? Would you like to use your real name?

15.40 GMT

> *i like to use my real name*, but unfortunately to make customer feel that he is talking to a real English guy, we need to use English names.
>
> 20.48 PKT

do you wish the customers were more open-minded?

16.07 GMT

> it eases the conversation if customer is more open minded.
>
> 21.08 PKT

how do you find the customers generally? are they polite or rude?

16.10 GMT

> Most of the customers now are polite, and a few are rude
>
> 21.11 PKT

do you think the company tries to hide your identity in some way?

16.12 GMT

> yes and thats a bad thing
>
> 21.13 PKT

> i agree. can you expand a little more?
> 16.14

i always feel bad about hiding my name, and why should i? if i am saadia then i am Saadia and not Anna or Elsa or Nicky etc
21.17 PKT

> I agree. Does it make you feel invisible?
> 16.17 GMT

Yes it does as we do not see the customer face to face
21.18 PKT

> When you speak with clients from UK they doesn't know that you are based in Pakistan right?
> 16.22 GMT

Yes they do not know that we are based in pakistan
21.30 PKT

> Do you feel any particular relationship between the UK and Pakistan?
> 16.32 GMT

many immigrants in UK are from Pakistan. We were under British rule for around 100 years, yes UK has deep roots here in sub continent
21.41 PKT

> With all these things, for example: having to lie while working, being outsourced by other companies for cheap-labour, not having opportunities for finding the job you would like to have. Would you like to live in another country? And if yes, which one?
> 16.43 GMT

Australia, UK and Canada as per my priorities

and i am trying it also

It gives a sad feeling to me that my country is wasting huge potential resources and they are all leaving the country
21.41 PKT

...

11   *Us* (drawing), 2022, blue pen on graph paper, 210mm x 297mm

12   *Us* (framed), 2022, blue pen on graph paper and pink post it on a file folder. 660cm x 491cm x 5cm

> is it easy for you to go to the UK? Since you have worked already for the UK?
>
> 16.45 GMT

i have worked for UK but not in UK and thats why its difficult for me to move there

21.45 PKT

> Fake globalisation
>
> 16.50 GMT

immigration policies are also not relaxed as compared to Canada

21.51 PKT

> even if you were colonised by the UK, don't you get any help?
>
> well... side effects of colony — amnesia
>
> they come, take, leave and forget
>
> 16.51 GMT

Yeah they came took, tore us apart and leave but thats history now. We need to live in present and think for the future. UK is motherland of many Pakistanis and Indians now.

21.57 PKT

> I agreed with you. We can't live in the past otherwise we won't progress. The problem is that we need to be aware of the past in order to change the present
>
> 16.58 GMT

i agree and this is a fake globalisation

its all about money everywhere, there is nothing like development, human development and rest of the quality stuff

22.01 PKT

> That's right. Do you think is a problem of corruption within Pakistan or is it more about UK requesting labour for lower prices?
>
> 17.02 GMT

The problem is at both ends as UK should sign agreements mentioning minimum wage and ensuring it but they don't do it

22.06 PKT

> so in general term do you feel that UK companies has been good to people outsourced in Pakistan (currently)
>
> 17.12 GMT

The terms that UK companies negotiate with Pakistani companies to outsource just need an addition of minimum wage at least to 400 pounds or equivalent rest all is fine with me

We are being paid very less here

our monthly wage can go maximum of 200 pounds inclusive of commissions

22.15 PKT

> that's important to know
>
> my god that's nothing
>
> 17.15 GMT

Exactly!

22.17 PKT

> can live ok with that in there?
>
> having for example two kids?
>
> can you leave with that money?
>
> 17.18 GMT

only kids do not work and rest all family members need to earn

then we can make an acceptable living and even not a decent one

how do you feel about call centres especially an outsourced one?

22.19 PKT

> I'm not sure really
>
> I feel bad that Pakistani workers are gettting paid a fraction of what they would earn in the UK
>
> 17.20 GMT

UK companies may be are paying a better rate per agent but its Pakistani outsourced companies which are giving very lesser rate to agents.

...

that's a great idea

I was wondering if you are getting pay for this? Cause if not it'd be ironic

It would

17.32 GMTh

> i wish i could tell people how different it is, than normal call centre jobs.
>
> 22.33 PKT

So that means that you are getting fairly paid for participating here?

17.36 GMT

> Here, Yes! but as an agent in Call Centre for an outsourced company, No!
>
> 22.36 PKT

I am glad to hear that

how do you imagine your job will change in the future?

17.37 GMT

> it will change for sure as it has been so far, i will also change with it, adapt new technologies and move on

> i feel they should pay us good in return and thats all

> we are all good workers, we sacrifice our social and personal life, sleep, family and many other things for companies and at the end of the day we get peanuts only
>
> 22.38 PKT

wow, sorry to hear that. I imagine how difficult it must be to deal with that day by day.

17.40 GMT

> they spread such rumours just to keep us scary

> But i wonder how can we change it
>
> 22.41 PKT

do you have any sort of union or way of organising together?

17.42 GMT

> its a good idea, many people have asked me same thing but this might not help

as the only constant thing in call centre is hiring and firing

There is no such union

if we leave they will hire fresh people

they will get more cheap labour

22.44 PKT

Do you think they use that threat to coerce or control you in some way?

17.46 GMT

Yes they do

they openly say if you dont want to work we will hire more people, infact hiring and firing never stops in call centres

22.44 PKT

and is being made unemployed a scary prospect?

17.45 GMT

unemployed to set an example and scare other workers

fear of losing a job is one of the scariest things here

22.49 PKT

what would happen to you if you lost your job

17.50 GMT

i have a family to feed and this dilema never changes for each one of us working in my capacity

we dont want to lose it but we are also not satisfied with what they pay us

22.50 PKT

i understand. it's very hard.

17.51 GMT

Yes it is

22.51 PKT

we've all gotta make that $$$

17.52 GMT

Yes and that's why we are being treated as machines and not humans

22.56 PKT

do you feel like a machine then?
18.03 GMT

how would you feel if you chat with 7/8 people at the same time

you cannot even check your cell phone, cannot answer phone and even cannot have lunch
23.06 PKT

whoa sounds exhausting
18.08 GMT

and to keep that smile on the face all the time :)

at the end of the day its our job and we have to do it right
23.11 PKT

is there another job you'd like to have that was less stressful
18.12 GMT

There are very less opportunities and a huge crowd waiting for jobs outside, those who has job feel proud of it and want to keep it so we are all scary
23.13 PKT

so you have to hold onto a job whatever the cost
18.14 GMT

Yes thats what the situation demands here
23.15 PKT

so do you feel more worried about being fired for doing something wrong than losing your job to automation
18.15 GMT

Alas! Yes automation is a fear, doing something wrong and getting fired is also a fear, there're multiple things going on at the same time in this industry, rumours like "we might lose this project from next month" is also a fear
23.16 PKT

do you think they use those fears to make you not question decisions the managers make?
18.22 GMT

> Yes!
> 23.24 PKT

So you've been working in the call centre industry for quite some time

What are some of the strangest things you've experienced in your job?
18.28 GMT

> Outsourcing, Pay cuts, third party contracts, cost optimization (Cost Cutting) and many more
> 23.29 PKT

What exactly happens in cost optimization?
18.29 GMT

> they cut operation costs by laying off people, by cutting some facilities.
> 23.31 PKT

If you want to study in the university? Do you need to work at the same time to be able to pay your studies?
18.32 GMT

> Yes we study and work to support our own studies.
> 23.33 PKT

Where did you do your masters in sociology?
18.34 GMT

> From University of Punjab, Pakistan
> 23.35 PKT

Ah nice!

You are highly qualified – has your degree helped you in your work?
18.36 GMT

> Well! in Pakistan Call Center jobs are considered as part time jobs or a person who does not get any suitable job can get a Call Center job at any stage of his life
> 23.40 PKT

Do you enjoy your job?
18.41 GMT

> Yea i do but its hectic
> 23.41 PKT

...

How is the work pressure? Do you have to speak to a minimum amount of customers per day?
18.42 GMT

its immense as we need to talk to around 300 customers per day in 8 hours
23.43 PKT

WOW

And what happens if you don't speak to 300 customers in that time?
18.44 GMT

our service level gets hurt

and that makes an impact on our salary
23.44 PKT

How realistic is it to speak to 300 customers in 8 hours?

Do most people manage to or not really?
18.45 GMT

its not managable

KPIs are not really realistic

they decreased the number many times but they again keep on increasing it
23.45 PKT

so does that mean most people get paycuts because of this?
18.46 GMT

yes
23.47 PKT

Wow...

And how many days do you work a week?
18.50 GMT

5 days in 1st week and 6 days in 2nd week
23.51 PKT

That's hectic indeed, as you said earlier
18.51 GMT

> yes it is but its life and one has to earn
>
> 23.52 PKT

absolutely

is there a way to grow in the company that you're working in at the moment?

18.55 GMT

> Honestly! i did not get job in my field and call centre is the only industry where you can find professionals from all disciplines, we have engineers, Drs and many others working in same capacity
>
> There is a promotion criteria and whoever meets it get promoted to next level after clearing test and interviews
>
> 23.56 PKT

What kind of field did you want to work in after finishing your MA?

18.57 GMT

> I have completer my Masters already
>
> 23.58 PKT

Yes, but what did you want to do instead of working in a call centre?

19.01 GMT

> and i am trying to get a job in NGOs but there is no hope as of yet
>
> 00.02 PKT

I'm sorry to hear that Saadia

19.03 GMT

> thats what it is
>
> 00.04 PKT

Imagine it's similar for a lot of your colleagues

19.06 GMT

> Yes it is
>
> 00.07 PKT

do you usually work in call centres or also with live chats?

19.08 GMT

> Both
>
> 00.10 PKT

Ah

> With the live chats, do you have to speak to multiple customers at the same time?
>
> Or just one?
>
> 19.11 GMT

Right now i am talking to 3 including you and yes sometimes the number goes upto 7/8

00.12 PKT

> Whoa, all at the same time
>
> 19.15 GMT

Yes all at the same time

00.16 PKT

> can i ask if any people around you experience burn-outs from work?
>
> 19.16 GMT

Yes you can... and burn out is one common issue that we all face but we *keep on smiling* thats how we are trained

fig. 13,14   43,44

00.16 PKT

> during your time working there, what have you most learned about human behaviour / people?
>
> A big question I know! haha
>
> 19.18 GMT

Wow! a really big question

Well! people are different and i believe its because of certain things like culture, education and demographics of the area

People from UK behave in a certain manner, USA are different, Norwegians are different and same goes for us Pakistanis and Indians

What do you think about outsourcing of Call Centers and how do you feel about that expecially with things like time difference and different culture

00.19 PKT

> Cultural differences are really interesting in this way
>
> ...

As we move more into digital forms of conversation (this as an example) – I think its increasingly important that we have a sense of the people we are talking to on the other side of the screen. Having seen your biography before talking to you, gives me small sense of your voice and identity. This has a huge impact on the type of conversation we then have

Of course, call centres have a very specific purpose / customer relationship

But without live voice, the LiveChat function needs to bring the human experience back in somehow

which is why I find this project interesting

19.23 GMT

> Very True!
>
> We have chatbots today. but trust me they really dont give that feel of human interaction during chats.
>
> 00.24 PKT

How have you learned to handle difficult conversations and dialogue? (if at all)

19.27 GMT

> A very good question indeed. 1st of all its our job and we need to serve every customer with a smile at our face and trust me, i am chatting with you and i have that smile on my face which you will see on any customer service center and we are given trainings for keeping such behaviors.
>
> it is difficult though! as we are also humans and mood swings are always there but we have strong quality checks on us and we need to give that feel to the customer which makes him comfortable and makes him think that he is at the right place.
>
> 00.28 PKT
>
> ...

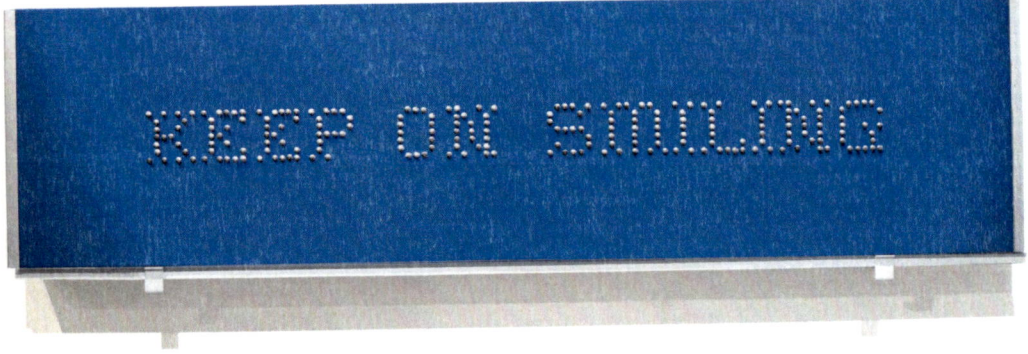

14 *Install shot (screen)*, 2022, How May I Serve You? SET Kensignton, London, UK.

15 *Keep on Smiling*, 2022, Screen divider made of wood, cotton fabric, stainless steel and incrustrated stainless steels pins. 200cm x 50cm x 5cm

> Difficult conversations always give us more learnings as we get to know if any such customer comes again in the future then we know how to handle.
>
> 00.28 PKT

Yeah I can imagine it is difficult to be consistently polite and engaging. It is a real skill and discipline

Why do you feel you need to smile? Is it because of habit?

19.30 GMT

> Smile is the most important thing, it keeps me confident and it helps me stay polite, humble and feel empathetic
>
> 00.31 PKT

But when you chat with you family do you always smile too?

19.31 GMT

> Hahahaha i keep that smile especially with my kids
>
> but of course, sometimes you get angry too
>
> 00.32 PKT

hahahahah

with kids it's better to keep the smile on

do you talk about your work with your kids sometimes?

19.38 GMT

> yeah i do
>
> they must know how difficult is to earn
>
> its my job to smile even if i dont want to
>
> so thats an art
>
> 00.39 PKT

Yes that's very very hard

Do you have to follow a strict script?

19.39 GMT

> Very strict
>
> 00.40 PKT

> **what does it look like? is it a flow chart with different answer options?**
> 19.40 GMT

> oh no no, its kind of a standard operating procedure book, its always open with us and we need to seek help from it.
> 00.41 PKT

> **are you ever tempted to go off script?**
> 19.41 GMT

> We sometimes do! as sometimes we need to think out of the box to resolve customer's issue
> 00.42 PKT

> **does it ever feel like you would get in trouble if you go off script too much?**
> 19.42 GMT

> it happens, but i was never marked even if i went off the scripts as for us issue resolution is the main focus area
> 00.43 PKT

> **i see**
>
> **How visible do you feel as a worker?**
> 19.44 GMT

> very less!
>
> as we are always behind the screen. most people think that they are not really talking to a human and its a chatbot.
> 00.51 PKT

> **Ahh I understand, sorry to hear that!**
>
> **Do you think customers ever wonder about who is on the other end of the chat?**
> 19.51 GMT

> Most of the customers only want solution of their issue and they really dont care if its a human or a chatbot
>
> but some needs interaction with a real human
> 00.52 PKT

> You mean that it's important for some customers that there is a human on the other side of the screen?
>
> 19.52 GMT

Yes! not only for customers but for certain issues of the customers too

00.53 PKT

> That's interesting!
>
> Do you find customers can be rude sometimes? Why do you think that is?
>
> 19.54 GMT

customers get rude most of the time because they dont get solution of their issue

00.54 PKT

> Right, I'm sorry to hear. That sucks
>
> Has your job changed in significant ways since you started doing it?
>
> 19.55 GMT

Yeah! when i started it was different and as technology grew, new things kept coming in

00.55 PKT

> I see, have you noticed more tasks that you used to do are now being done by technology or computers?
>
> 19.55 GMT

technology has reduced the workload but at the same time it has increased the products too which makes it difficult for us to handle

00.57 PKT

> Oh right, and perhaps less people working because of technology?
>
> 19.57 GMT

Well number of people has also increased, salary has decreased :)

00.58 PKT

> Right, of course :(
>
> ...

> Do you foresee a situation where computers/technology take over your role completely?
> 19.58 GMT

i think they are already trying to inculcate artificial intelligence in our industry but humans role is also increasing with it
00.59 PKT

> That's interesting, so maybe they can't automate the jobs as much as they'd like?
> 19.59 GMT

you are correct
01.01 PKT

> Do you think there is anything that could be done to make customer service more human?
> 20.03 GMT

Control the churn rate of internal customers by paying them what they deserve and keeping them happy. You will keep your employees happy and they will definitely keep that human feel alive
01.04 PKT

> Right, keeping people feeling human sounds like the bare minimum that bosses could do

> Last couple of questions, I promise!

> I'm writing to you from London, and I'm wondering what your opinion of the UK is?
> 20.04 GMT

People of UK are good as there are many cultures living together.

with harmony and peace and thats the most important things
01.09 PKT

> That's true!

> Do you have a feel of hierarchy between you and UK citizens?
> 20.10 GMT

I belong to a poor country and yes there are many things which we feel deprived off

> Do you feel you are being exploited by countries like the UK?
>
> 20.12 GMT

Yes i do feel like that, as they pay less for outsourcing and then the employer in Pakistan pays even lesser to us for working with them

01.13 PKT

> Right, does all the talk of outsourcing and cheap labour feel dehumanising?
>
> 20.13 GMT

Yes its is...

as one end is saving money and the other end is making money with a compromise on what we need to get from them

01.14 PKT

> Yes, I understand
>
> What do you do during your days off? :)
>
> (I'm really enjoying this by the way, thank you so much <3)
>
> 20.14 GMT

thanks dear, during my off days i have lots of house chors to do then i have to spend looooooots of time with my kids specifically with my son coz he is too young

01.15 PKT

> Aw how old is he?
>
> Also do you have a favourite dish I should learn how to cook (I'm really into Pakistanese food)? :)
>
> 20.15 GMT

my son is 5 years old and my favourite dish is Pulao

01.17 PKT

> Ah exciting I'll look it up, thanks!
>
> what do you wish your kids to do when they get old?
>
> Sorry if this is too personnal
>
> You don't have to answer of course
>
> 20.18 GMT

> I just want them to follow their instinct, do not want to force anything on them. But definately no call centre jobs
>
> due to lesser salaries and other related things
>
> i dont want them to suffer
>
> 01.18 PKT

Of course I understand that

so in call center you make a lesser salary then most jobs in Pakistan?

20.19 GMT

> Yes that's how it is here
>
> 01.20 PKT

Why you don't want them to work in call centres?

And do you know why the salary is lower?? Seems insane to me?

20.21 GMT

> No personal life, no social life, lesser salaries, lesser commissions, very strict compliance and many more things
>
> 01.21 PKT

Why no personal and social life? Because of the schedules?

20.22 GMT

> Well our employers get paid a better rate per agent but they give us a very little amount out of it
>
> Can you imagine employing a person full time for 100 pounds per month
>
> 01.21 PKT

No I can't that sounds insane!

you make a 100£ a month?

20.23 GMT

> Yes, personal and social life gets impacted by the schedule. No weekends
>
> 01.23 PKT

> what is the median salary in Pakistan?
> 20.24 GMT

>> we get off on any day during the week
>> 01.25 PKT

> No weekend? How do you deal with your kids?
> This is very tough
> Who takes care of your kids when you are working usually?
> 20.26 GMT

>> My husband, he arranges his work schedule as per my schedule. if i am at home, he is at work and if he is at home, i am at work
>> 01.27 PKT

> Sorry if I'm annoying and you have to reply to me also haba
> so you never see each other?
> *hahaha
> 20.28 GMT

>> hahahaha
>> its not like that at least we see each other twice or thrice in a week for few hours
>> 01.28 PKT

> Do you normally work more than 8hours per day?
> 20.29 GMT

>> Yes
>> 01.31 PKT

> How many more?
> 20.32 GMT

>> A mother :)
>> its 24 hours
>> 01.32 PKT

> Hahahahaha true
> and for the call center ? Haha
> 20.33 GMT

>> …

> 8 hours for Call Centre and then i keep searching for assignments for extra money

Okay

Another question – what are your hopes for the future? Another big question I'm sure haha

> Well! call centre industry was not at all my prime focus, when i was studying but now i find it interesting, things get worse sometimes as we dont get holidays on religious celebrations and other important ceremonies
>
> but still i have a job!
>
> We have populated the world so much that its difficult to accomodate everyone

Of course. Thats an interesting point – you have to sync up so much to the rhythm and timings of your customers in other countries that you have to adjust your celebrations and holidays

> Exactly
>
> This industry is very good but with the rapid pace growth in technology and more money, we are being treated as slaves
>
> More revenues is the only concern of employers
>
> i think they should sign contracts with outsourced companies by deciding a minimum wage that should attract and retain the agent
>
> and you asked about median salary its around 150 to 200 USD here

And you make 100£ is that the minimum wage or not even?

Install shot (frames), 2022, How May I Serve You? SET Kensington, London, UK. 16

Install shot (stool), 2022, How May I Serve You? SET Kensington, London, UK. 17

BUT STILL I HAVE A JOB

18   *Till* (drawing), 2022, blue pen on graph paper, 210mm x 297mm

19   *Till* (framed), 2022, blue pen on graph paper and pink post it on a file folder. 660cm x 491cm x 5cm

> Yes! that's what i make
> 01.47 PKT

What are the facilities like at the places that you work in?
20.48 GMT

> Pick n drop facility (Females Only), medical (Very little), maternity leaves
> 01.48 PKT

And you get picked up and dropped off in order to get to work and back home safely, right?
20.49 GMT

> yes thats the biggest facility i feel
> 01.49 PKT

Would it be really unsafe for you if you had to get to work without this?
20.50 GMT

> no not at all but it saves me cost of travelling
> 01.50 PKT

Ah, I see! So how come the transport is only organised for women and not for men?
20.51 GMT

> because of the schedule
>
> sometimes we get to work at night, sometimes in the evenings and at times in the mornings
>
> its a rotational shift job
> 01.52 PKT

Makes sense

oh and I was also wondering if there are more women working your job than men or not really?

Or like also hierarchy is it more men in higher position and women in lower ones?

Sorry for jumping questions like this
20.53 GMT

> In Pakistan women prefer call centre jobs and there are many working in this industry

> in hierarchy there are more men and a few women in upper management level
>
> but there is an open merit system, they see good performers and take tests, interviews and promote them accordingly.
>
> 01.59 PKT

Thats good but do men usually work more for example bc they don't have to take care of the children as much?

Or something like this or not necessarily?

sorry just asking bc I don't believe in merit bc there are so many biases in the world

21.00 GMT

> Yeah men work more as if i spend 8 hours a day in office, i see men spending 12 to 14 hours daily in office, learning and grooming and bringing in new things
>
> 02.02 PKT

like women get taken less seriously, they have to sometimes quit their work and stop their career bc they have kids

makes sense

this is the same in so many industries tho

sorry for my feminist rant

21.03 GMT

> Well don't be, you are absolutely on the same page where i am
>
> our prime focus is our family and that's why we feel satisfied for what we do
>
> 02.04 PKT

Exactly
21.06 PKT

> its very difficult, as a mother i have to take care of a lot of things for them but thee schedule really makes me tire everyday but again i have to put that smile back on my face to get the life running
>
> 02.11 PKT

Of course mother usually have more to take on at home as well

specially if there's kids
21.12 GMT

> Very true!
> 02.12 PKT

smile is also something asked a lot of women

do customers ever ask for your personal information?
21.13 GMT

> Yes they do
>
> its a very common thing that we del in every 3rd chat/call
>
> especially for females
> 02.14 PKT

wow

what do they ask for?
21.15 GMT

> Where do you live?
>
> what is you number?
>
> will you be my friend?
>
> you are very beautiful (how would you get an idea about beauty through voice or text)
>
> some scolds, some abuse
> 02.15 PKT

and you're not allowed to answer those questions, right?

(not that you'd want to i would imagine)
21.16 GMT

> Hahahah
>
> Yes we are not allowed and we also dont want to :)
>
> 02.16 PKT

lol! :)

yeah must be creepy to get guys asking you that all the time

every 3rd call... so often!
21.20 GMT

> Again! thats human nature
>
> 02.21 PKT

yeah i guess!
21.20 GMT

> whats your profession?
>
> 02.21 PKT

student still

studying graphic design
21.22 GMT

> Oh great so you will be beautifying the world that we see on computers
>
> any weired experience about customer services?
>
> 02.23 PKT

hahahah i take that as a compliment thx

hmm not really

just they sometimes can't really solve my problem
21.24 GMT

> Awww thats true
>
> sometimes we cannot get out of the policies and we cannot tell the truth to customer
>
> just false promises but thats what we are told to do
>
> 02.24 PKT

ah i see
21.25 GMT

> Due to some crank customers we think others genuine customers are also crank

> so sometimes we are unable to serve due to a bad experience in previous call coz its hard to take the stuff from your mind in seconds
>
> but still we are trained and managed to do so
>
> 02.26 PKT

cranky customers, ufff

im sorry

21.26 GMT

> Yeah! especially with female customer service representatives
>
> 02.27 PKT

yea people should show more sympathy

21.28 GMT

> problem with our world is that we have more judgemental people around and less observers
>
> 02.29 PKT

did you feel emotional impacts from those weird/crank conversation?

21.29 GMT

> sometimes we even feel broken and we do cry as well, many of us has taken calls or served customers with tears in their eyes
>
> 02.30 PKT

omg i'm sorry

21.31 GMT

> not your fault at all
>
> sometimes it feels like what am i doing here? i should just leave the place immediately
>
> but what can i do, thats my job
>
> 02.32 PKT

true..

What subjects did you like as a child?

11.16 GMT

> i liked languages most and later on psychology was my favourite one

> which one is yours
>
> 16.18 PKT

> What languages did you like?

> And what part of psychology were you interested in?
>
> 11.19 GMT

> english, urdu, persian
>
> 16.20 PKT

> I enjoyed art, history and english literature
>
> 11.20 GMT

> clinical psychology,

> it was back in 2011
>
> 16.25 PKT

> Your masters in sociology sounds really interesting - did you have a specialism during it?
>
> 11.26 GMT

> Thanks well i could not have any further time as i got married
>
> 16.28 PKT

> Ah I see, life happens hey!
>
> 11.30 GMT

> yeah true
>
> 16.30 PKT

> So is it almost midnight for you?
>
> 11.31 GMT

> yes, it's almost 12
>
> 16.31 PKT

> Earlier when I was typing about your masters you preemptively answered saying 'it was back in 2011'

> can you see what we type before sending?
>
> 11.33 GMT

> Yes i can see what you are typing as it helps me to prepare my answer earlier and make the conversation quicker
>
> 16.34 PKT

> ...

> Oh wow, i had no idea
>
> then in theory we could a conversation without me never sending a message
>
> 11.41 GMT

hahahahaha thats true

16.41 PKT

> so good
>
> does that mean you ever see people typing thihngs that they never send?
>
> frustrations etc
>
> 11.43 GMT

yes!

but we never tell them that we know

because their frustration is not something i can do anything about , my job is toresolve their issues and thats what i am here to do

16.45 PKT

> yes that makes sense
>
> and perhaps they would see it as invasive
>
> but im sorry if that leads to you seeing things that people do not intend for you to see
>
> 11.46 GMT

it does not matter even if we see it as we never disclose it and this feature is only there to keep the conversation quick and let us serve more customers

16.47 PKT

> can i ask you another question?
>
> 11.47 GMT

sure

16.48 PKT

> what has been your most memorable call centre story? like a customer you will never forget
>
> 11.50 GMT

> my husband 😮
>
> 16.52 PKT

what?!

really?

11.53 GMT

> Yes! We talked through call center and tied the knot
>
> 16.54 PKT

no way! thats amazing

11.55 GMT

> Yes thats true
>
> now we have 4 kids
>
> 16.57 PKT

wow - a modern love story

11.59 GMT

> hahahaha true
>
> 17.00 PKT

what did your friends think?

were they skeptical at first?

12.01 GMT

> No, there was nothing like that
>
> it was just a general conversation and it just happened afterwards
>
> we even stopped talking for a year or so but destiny
>
> 17.04 PKT

oh wow ! yeah when you find your person and its your person

12.05 GMT

> Yeah true. We share the dream of travelling the whole world
>
> 17.08 PKT

Where would you start your trip?

12.11 GMT

> from Makkah Saudi Arabia
>
> 17.13 PKT

How come you would like to start there?

12.15 GMT

> ...

> thats our religious place i would go and perform my religious duty first and then move on
>
> 17.18 PKT

Where woul you like to end?

12.18 GMT

> Scotland
>
> for a peaceful living as Scotland has a wonderful countryside
>
> 17.20 PKT

It does yeah, we have just travelled there

its quite remarkable

12.21 GMT

> no doubt! God has created a beautiful world and we humans have spoiled it
>
> 17.24 PKT

and the cities in Scotland are beautiful

12.24 GMT

> true, I imagine
>
> 17.25 PKT

What is islamabad like?

12.25 GMT

> its a very beautiful city, full of nature, trees, mountains, small dams
>
> once you live in Islamabad, no other city is good enough
>
> 17.25 PKT

Iv just googled

it looks amazing

12.26 GMT

> Yes it is
>
> you should visit us here
>
> 17.26 PKT

I would love too

Btw, are you into music?

what's your favorite song?

12.28 GMT

> Ed Shreen Perfect

> that's a great song
>
> is he popular in pakistan?
>
> 12.31 GMT

Yes he is, such polite voice and magical lyrics

17.32 PKT

> he does have a nice voice ! I like the version with Beyonce
>
> 12.33 GMT

I wonder why you asked this question as i was listening to him

17.33 PKT

> oh really? ha!
>
> i should listen to him more
>
> 12.34

yeah Thinking Out Loud

17.35 PKT

> a classic ! think my fave ed shereran song is probably \Shape of You
>
> 12.35 GMT

yeah thats another masterpiece

17.36 PKT

> or Galway Girl
>
> Anyway i have to go now, it was really nice chatting to you
>
> enjoy the ed sheeran !
>
> 12.36 GMT

same here

thanks for your time

17.38 PKT

> Saadia, before I go, do you need anything from me?
>
> 12.37 GMT

Anything Like?

17.39 PKT

> anything
>
> 12.40 GMT

Just prayers and nothing else

however if you want to know anything about call centre outsourcing, please feel free to ask

17.41 PKT

ok I'll pray

with love

Hey Saadia, thank you for taking your time. It's been a pleasure talking to you

Enjoy your evening. I hope it brings a cooler breeze!

12.44 PKT

        it was really nice talking to you too

        Thank You! have a nice weekend!

        17.46 PKT

Live chat
Malik Ayaz

Transcripts
José García Oliva

#

greetings (p.72) weather (72) sport (72) politics (73,76) wage (74,88,94,104) animals (74) tourism (75) cubicles (77) toneofvoice (78,91) breaks (79) monitoring (79) workconditions (79,89,90,99) destiny (87) studies (87) outsourcing (88,90) unions (89) covid (90) family (91) migration (92) automation (93) identity (95) racism (97) awareness (110) farewell (111)

fig.

20	*Install shot (cubicles)*	p.80
21	*Install shot (computer)*	80,81
22	*Audience 01*	82
23	*Audience 02*	82
24	*Audience 03*	82
25	*Audience 04*	83
26	*Audience 05*	83
27	*Audience 06*	83
28	*Screen divider (photos) 1/2*	84
29	*Screen divider (mirror)*	84,85
30	*Screen divider (photos) 2/2*	85
31	*Well Behaved*	102
32	*Framed c*	103
33	*Untitled (perfect lovers) 1/2*	106
34	*Website (PKT-GMT time zone)*	106
35	*Untitled (perfect lovers) 2/2*	107
36	*Time zones map*	108,109

On the following pages, you will find a selection of the conversations between visitors and Malik Ayaz. The chats have been shortened and connected from one discussion to another in order to keep continuity in the subject matter and improve the writing flow. The chat order hasn't changed, and all the words were kept the same, including colloquialism, acronyms and misspellings.

London, United Kingdom Islamabad, Pakistan
Customer Malik Ayaz

> Hello, how may I help you?
> 18.21 PKT

Hello! How are you?

Nice to meet you

12.22 GMT

> I'm good, how are you?
> 18.22 PKT

I'm good! it's nice weather where I am and I want to go and play cricket but I have work to do.

How's the weather there?

13.23 GMT

> The weather is Cold here
> 18.25 PKT

This is a standard English opener for any conversation!

13.25 GMT

> I never knew that
> 18.28 PKT

Oh haha yeah and it's very important to the English to complain about the weather no matter what. It's like a type of solidarity and sharing

13.29 GMT

> hahahaha..... thats good way to start a conversation
> 18.29 PKT

Do you like cricket?

13.29 GMT

> I am fond of cricket and in the past I have been a very good batsman.
> 18.29 PKT

Probably much better than me.

I used to play when I was younger but haven't for a long time

...

72

> but I am visiting my family at the moment and played recently with my brothers

> I was very slow!

13.30 GMT

> recently lost final from you guys

18.31 PKT

> hehehe i know

13.31 GMT

> you are new t20 champs

18.31 PKT

> i know! we're great!

13.31 GMT

> Yeah! Great Great Britians

18.32 PKT

> well, Stokes is

13.32 GMT

> well doesn't matter UK is like 2nd home to many of Pakistanis so in fact the cup remained at home

18.33 PKT

> hahaaha that is a wonderful way to look at this

13.33 GMT

> we need to find ways to find and maintain peace

> instead of spreading hattered

18.33 PKT

> Was it big news in pakistan, that the london mayor Sadiq Khan, is from Pakistani heritage?

> that is a beautiful mantra

13.35 GMT

> Actually it feels like the Colonizer is being colonized by having people from Pakistan, India and Bangladesh in UKs Parliament

> sounds great that people from sub continent are progressing there

> whats your take on it
> 18.36 PKT

It's great we've got greater diversity and representation in parliament

And Malik just so that I know, are you getting paid for doing this?
13.36 GMT

> Yes! I am getting paid for doing this.
> 18.37 PKT

OK, OK. I'm glad to hear this.

How has it been so far?
13.38 GMT

> It has been wonderful as of now
>
> And it's quite interesting to tell people how we work and what are the challenges that we face.
> 18.39 PKT

I imagine! For once you can voice your opinion outside the boundaries of your company!

I need to know about your favourite animal.
13.40 GMT

> My favourite animal is the ibex
> 18.40 PKT

Oh wow!

I've just googled it –

They are amazing.
13.41 GMT

> Yes! They are, and the speed they climb is amazing
> 18.41 PKT

I imagine.
13.42 GMT

> They live on mountain ranges like the Himalaya and Karakoram.
> 18.42 PKT

Are you close to those regions?
13.43 GMT

> Yes, I live in Pakistan and we have highest mountain ranges of the world here –
>
> Himalaya, Karakoram and Hindu Kush,
>
> one of the best places for tourism.
> 18.44 PKT

I know, I heard recently that the Himalaya was getting saturated with human poop

Because of all the climbers.
13.44 GMT

> True!
> 18.45 PKT

Damn, that is kind of a pity.

Tourism can be a double-edged sword.

Do you climb?
13.46 GMT

> Yeah, that's one of my hobbies
>
> But not that much as you I feel
> 18.46 PKT

Must be very beautiful climbing those mountains

Except for the poop
13.46 GMT

> It's animal poop mostly
> 18.47 PKT

I heard a lot about Europeans going to Pakistan backpacking in the 60s 70s
13.48 GMT

> and now Pakistanis are backpacking and want to leave for anywhere but Pakistan
>
> 18.50 PKT

What has changed? Is it economy, politics, religion, ecology, everything?

13.51 GMT

> economy is in crisis
>
> political destability
>
> corruption and what not
>
> Why did you ask about my favourite animal ?
>
> 18.51 PKT

That is the question I ask everyone I meet.

Mostly when I'm drunk, but also any regular day

13.52 GMT

> Hahahaha, so are you drunk or it's just another regular day?
>
> 18.52 PKT

Regular day.

13.53 GMT

> OK.
>
> You are one interesting customer that has brought a smile to my face. Thanks!
>
> 18.53 PKT

Happy to help!

Happy to serve you, hahaha.

13.54 GMT

> Yeah! Happy to help!
>
> So what would you like to know about call centres?
>
> 18.55 PKT

> My question has always been what the physical architecture of a call center is like. Are you all in one big room? What environment do you live in?
>
> (My MA degree is architecture :)
>
> 13.58 GMT

Good question!

We all sit in a big hall, with soundproofing on the walls, and have our own cubicles.

19.02 PKT

> how many people you work with?
>
> like how many people in your room
>
> cuz i got the impression from films
>
> there like hundred of ppl in a room
>
> 14.03 GMT

we have 2 big halls and at one single point in time we have around 200 logins

19.04 PKT

> means 200 ppl in a room?
>
> 14.05 GMT

total headcount is around 800

200 in a very big hall/room

we are divided into teams

one team consists of 15 to 20 members

and 10 to 12 teams are logged in at the same time

and this depends upon the nature of the project too

if the project needs 5 to 10 agents then we schedule them accordingly

> Normally Telecom call centers are very bid as they have a high influx of calls
>
> 19.05 PKT

ohh make sense

14.06 GMT

> When one agent finishes his shift then the other can utilise that particular cubicle.
>
> 19.06 PKT

Do you see each other, or are the cubicles solid surfaces?

Do you switch places also, after Covid?

14.07 GMT

> They are made of wood, and we can see each other: in a few call centres we have mirrors in place right in front of us so that we can see our facial expressions while talking to customers and keep our selves smiling all the time..
>
> 19.08 PKT

fig. 20,21,29   80,81,85

Interesting, the mirror device.

14.08 GMT

> Indeed it is :)
>
> 19.09 PKT

I can relate to it now that we are all digital. It is really easy to be serious when you don't have another human being in front of you

14.10 GMT

> Exactly!
>
> 19.11 PKT

Do you also have training in the tone of voice, pace, etc?

14.11 GMT

> Yes, that's one integral part, we listen to extremely polite and calls in a soft tone and relate this to our tone and pace...
>
> ...and then adopt what's necessary to improve our quality of tone, pitch, pace and voice.
>
> 19.12 PKT

> How is it to be working behind a screen for long hours? Are you working more than eight hours?
>
> ?
>
> 14.14 GMT

> It's difficult and hectic also but we have training for it and try to manage it as it does not give a real feel of a face-to-face conversation so we need to ensure that it gives a proper feel of a face-to-face conversation as much as possible.
>
> 19.14 PKT

> I can imagine... It sounds difficult.
>
> Do you have enough breaks during the day?
>
> 14.15 GMT

> Two breaks of fifteen minutes and one of thirty minutes for a meal but we need to manage it within time as we are monitored through the software.
>
> 19.16 PKT

> Is it true that when you work in customer service chats you are supervised including everything you are saying? Is this mentally healthy? Being observed constantly?
>
> Those breaks are within the eight-hour shift? Or is it less than that?
>
> 14.16 GMT

> Yes, that's true. We are monitored all the time and that's not mentally healthy but one has to earn.
>
> We listen to recorded conversations to improve the quality of our services
>
> 19.20 PKT

20	*Install shot (cubicles)*, 2022, How May I Serve You? SET Kensignton, London, UK.
21	*Install shot (desktop)*, 2022, How May I Serve You? SET Kensignton, London, UK.
22	*Audience 01 (performance)*, 2022, How May I Serve You? SET Kensignton, London, UK.
23	*Audience 02 (performance)*, 2022, How May I Serve You? SET Kensignton, London, UK.
24	*Audience 03 (performance)*, 2022, How May I Serve You? SET Kensignton, London, UK.
25	*Audience 04 (performance)*, 2022, How May I Serve You? SET Kensignton, London, UK.
26	*Audience 05 (performance)*, 2022, How May I Serve You? SET Kensignton, London, UK.
27	*Audience 06 (performance)*, 2022, How May I Serve You? SET Kensignton, London, UK.

22

23

24

25

26

27

Screen divider (photos) 1/2, 2022, How May I Serve You? SET Kensignton, London, UK.	28
Screen divider (mirror), 2022, How May I Serve You? SET Kensignton, London, UK	29
Screen divider (photos) 2/2, 2022, How May I Serve You? SET Kensignton, London, UK	30

> Is it possible instead of checking the agent's performance constantly, to have a system in place that is based on trust and letting the other person solve their problem themselves? Or do you think people make too many mistakes?

14.24 GMT

> > Well we are monitored by systems but they allow our Team Leaders and Supervisors to keep checking on us, they can listen to us while we are talking to customers, they can see our chats, and they can listen to the recordings later.

> > All these things are to ensure quality assurance

19.25 PKT

> I don't like it, it means people on the phone or helping you in chats

> Are always controlled

> There can't be space for human error.

14.26 GMT

> > Any human error in our job is considered a mistake and we get penalised for that in terms of pay cuts

19.27 PKT

> :(

> You should get training, not pay cuts

14.28 GMT

> > I was demoted once due to a small mistake but fortunately I got three promotions in a row after that, God is always kind and he finds a way out of nowhere.

> >

> It's an art to keep yourself energetic and passionate for each new interaction with a different customer every day and it's difficult and hectic
>
> 19.31 PKT

I'm sure.

Is this what you have always wanted to do?

14.31 GMT

> Things have changed a lot over the past few years due to the rapid growth in technology
>
> 19.32 PKT

Oh yeah?

14.33 GMT

> during start of my career it was SMS, as people use to chat through texting via SMS
>
> then GPRS to 3G to 4G and now 5G
>
> people call more for information on new products now
>
> 19.34 PKT

Oh, so interesting

14.35 GMT

> facebook, twitter, instagram and all such platforms
>
> I never wanted to do this but I believe it was my destiny so I accepted it.
>
> 19.36 PKT

You believe it's part of a wider plan for your pathway?

14.36 GMT

> I graduated in Computing and then got a job in a call centre during my study and since then I haven't been able to get out of it
>
> 19.37 PKT

Oh, interesting.

What was it that draw you to computers?

14.37 GMT

> was inclined towards programing but unfortunately could not find a career in that industry.
>
> 19.38 PKT

That's such a shame.

14.39 GMT

> Yes, it is.
>
> 19.40 PKT

OK, but I guess with the ever-changing shifts that makes it quite hard to concentrate on programming when you get home

14.40 GMT

> I don't do it anymore, it's really hard to find time for family in this job
>
> 19.41 PKT

Of course.

On a slightly different note, in an ideal world, how would you change these outsourcing mechanisms?

What would you do differently?

I imagine other people are also asking you existential questions.

14.42 GMT

> i would have deployed a member of staff from the UK to Pakistan to ensure proper compliance with the agreement; I would have asked the reasons for the high turnover rate of employees and the lower salaries.
>
> I would have tried to retain my employees
>
> 19.42 PKT

Are they not retaining their employees?

Why do you think there is a high turnover rate of employees and the low salaries?

14.43 GMT

> The low salary is the main reason for the high turnover.
>
> The salary is way too low
>
> 19.43 PKT

> They need to pay you more!
>
> 14.44 GMT

> A UK company outsources a Pakistani company to reduce its cost, the Pakistani company in turn focuses on making money out of what they get from UK
>
> So if they agree on a salary of £400 in the agreement, they would pay a maximum of £200 to employees.
>
> 19.44 PKT

> OK, so basically the employee doesn't get anything in this exchange – or not much
>
> Why aren't there organised unions to try and help the workers' rights?
>
> do you, as workers, have any forum between you to dicuss things like this?
>
> 14.45 GMT

> No, there is no such forum
>
> That's one very fine question, and what they do is, they scare us, by threatening we'll lose our job, lose projects and other stuff like that, spreading rumours to keep us constantly scared.
>
> 19.45 PKT

> But how come the workers' rights get abused like this without no repercussions
>
> ?
>
> And how does it make you feel?
>
> 14.46 GMT

> It's always painful

> I know people who served in this industry and later they were forced to resign and they are still unemployed.
>
> 19.47 PKT

That's terrible!

14.48 GMT

> thats life in this part of the world
>
> 19.48 PKT

Do you think it's okay for UK companies to outsource these types of services in countries like Pakistan?

Because the reason they outsource is because it's cheaper for them, but then how can Pakistan ever rise to the same economic level of the UK?

14.49 GMT

> Outsourcing is always good as cost optimisation is a company's right but manipulation on the other hand is wrong – they just need to ensure compliance to the agreements they are making with Pakistani companies.
>
> i even think that now there is no need to outsource to call centres
>
> You can hire people remotely and pay them and can save more money.
>
> It's easy to work from home, Covid has given many reasons for humans to rethink our approach to life. We can optimise more if we hire people directly from the UK/USA and pay them a fair wage, instead of filling the pockets of one single company or individual
>
> 19.53 PKT

Yes, Covid has changed many things.

> By the way – random question, but do you feel like you have to change your language usually when you work? Is it partly scripts, or?
>
> 14.54 GMT

> We used to change our language according to different accents
>
> In our industry they call it matching the customer level
>
> 19.55 PKT

> Matching the customer level sounds like a term that is very denigrating but hidden under polite wording
>
> 14.56 GMT

> Yes that's right.
>
> 19.56 PKT

> how do you manage to be constantly smiling and polite when you're talking to people?
>
> I personally couldn't do it.
>
> 14.57 GMT

> i was not like this eighteen years ago when i joined this industry, but with plenty of training, plenty of calls every day i have changed 360 degrees.
>
> 19.57 PKT

> Ok OK, so you think is a matter of experience?
>
> Do you have kids?
>
> 14.58 GMT

> Yes,
>
> Two girls and a boy.
>
> 20.01 PKT

> Oh, that's so nice! How old are they?
>
> Do you talk about your job with them?
>
> 15.03 GMT

> Nine, seven and five – and yes i talk about my job with them.
>
> 20.02 PKT

What do they say about your job?

15.03 GMT

> Sometimes kids say the most honest things, haha.
>
> 20.03 PKT

Would you recommend your kids to work in a call centre if they asked you?

15.04 GMT

> I would recommend them to join the army instead of joining my profession :)
>
> As both are the same
>
> With no personal life and always being available
>
> For the job.
>
> 20.05 PKT

That's tough.

If you could live in another country, which would you move to?

15.06 GMT

> Canada, the UK, Norway and Netherlands are also good, but immigration policies are strict for us.
>
> 20.06 PKT

If you could live in another country, How do you feel when you work for a country that you cannot be in?

15.07 GMT

> It's always good! i get to know people, I get to know the culture, it increases my education and that's always something good
>
> 20.08 PKT

And how long have you been doing the job?

15.09 GMT

> For the last eighteen years
>
> 20.10 PKT

A long time!

15.10 GMT

> Indeed.
> 20.10 PKT

So has the role changed in the last few years in line with technological change?
15.11 GMT

> The more I went up the ladder, things became different, there are more opportunities at a starting-level position than at director level or management position and technology has played a vital role in making the roles of supervisors and managers obsolete.
> 20.12 PKT

And how has the work changed for you? Is it easier or harder now?
15.12 GMT

> It's harder now.
>
> Even now we have new systems, more powerful, more intelligent, quicker.
>
> But the workload has increased dramatically over the past few years.
> 20.15 PKT

Does it feel like the human agents will be replaced by the machines?
15.15 GMT

> Chatbots are already there.
>
> And soon we will see that they might interact as humans.
> 20.17 PKT

Does that worry you?
15.17 GMT

> Not at all! I know there will be more products for us to sell.
> 20.18 PKT

You don't worry that humans will be automated out of the system?
15.18 GMT

> A chatbot does not yet know how to sell

...

> And that's what we humans can do better.

> Chatbots do not give a feeling of human interaction and they answer only pre-fed questions.
>
> 20.21 PKT

Do you think you work with more people now, or fewer than when you started?

15.22 GMT

> I work with more people now.

> When i started it was a 100-agent call centre and now it has around 1200
>
> 20.22 PKT

Wow.

And how often do people join or leave?

15.23 GMT

> There are 20 to 30 resignations every week,

> and the same amount of people joining in.
>
> 20.24 PKT

Wow, that is a big turnaround.

Why do people leave? And are there lots of people who want a job?

15.24 GMT

> People leave because of lower salaries,

> and there are many new people waiting just to gain a little experience.
>
> 20.25 PKT

Of course, that makes sense

Btw, how is your identity in these online services?

Do you think people that you interact with know where you are based?

15.25 GMT

> Most of them do not know where we are based as we never reveal our real names: mostly,

> we use English names while talking to customers in the UK and the USA.
>
> 20.28 PKT

But are your names translated or a completely different name?

15.29 GMT

> A completely different name,
>
> like Michael.
>
> 20.29 PKT

Wow, that's not nice at all... I thought that was a myth.

So you are forced to use another name to sound more English?

15.30 GMT

> Yes that's true.
>
> 20.31 PKT

Would you like to use your real name?

15.31 GMT

> I would always like to use my real name, but I cannot due to policy restrictions
>
> 20.32 PKT

Do you think the company tries to hide your identity a bit?

15.33 GMT

> They always want us to hide our identity.
>
> 20.34 PKT

Why do you think that is?

15.34 GMT

> Because the industry still feels that an English person would love to talk to an English person,
>
> they think it gives them a feeling that they are talking to someone who is their own kind.
>
> 20.35 PKT

Is it to make the customer feel more comfortable?

15.36 GMT

> Otherwise we are marked down in quality assurance and also have a pay cut.
>
> 20.36 PKT

Is there not legal help to make this stop happening? It feels completely unethical

that the agent is starting with a lie, just for the sake of making the customer feel at home?

15.37 GMT

> It is unethical, it should be banned, a company should own an outsourced function and a conversation starting with a lie is not at all a good thing.
>
> 20.38 PKT

Do you change the way you speak when speaking to English speakers?

15.39 GMT

> Yes I do, we always keep Mr. Google running with us :)
>
> 20.39 PKT

Haha.

15.40 GMT

> For vocabulary and other important stuff, we change the accent.
>
> 20.41 PKT

So do you change your accent then?

15.41 GMT

> Yeah.
>
> 20.42 PKT

How does it make you feel?

15.42 GMT

> It's just another part of my job and i am now used to it. We just spend two/three months on call and then we are ready for anything and adapt to any change.
>
> 20.43 PKT

And what about the profile picture?

Can you use a real one?

15.43 GMT

> We change that too :)
>
> 20.44 PKT

> And what are the profile pictures they use like? Is it like a clichéd handsome white man?
>
> 15.44 GMT

Yeah, that's exactly what we do.

20.45 PKT

> This is painful to hear.
>
> I'm imagining what it would be like to be in that position and it makes me question whether I'm feeling inferior...
>
> Like a third-class race, where we have to hide our own realities to please the white man
>
> 15.45 GMT

I am not white but I am proud of my colour.

That's one bitter reality of our world, but that's how it is.

20.46 PKT

> Have you felt racism towards you or your colleagues at work?
>
> 15.46 GMT

We all feel it, but we cannot do anything about it.

20.46 PKT

> Do you think with this kind of job is it possible to have a system in place where identity can be revealed, a fair salary offered, a non-racist atmosphere?
>
> Or do you think is it almost impossible if outsourcing exists?
>
> 15.47 GMT

Systems are already there and we just need to improve the way we outsource.

20.48 PKT

> Is it the responsibility of Pakistani companies or the foreign companies?
>
> 15.48 GMT

Corruption and love of money has left this country with nothing.

20.49 PKT

Do you think this way of seeing ourselves is something more about us (as if it is embedded within us) or is it how people from the West makes us feel?

I mean also advertising, films, visual history, basically.

15.49 GMT

> It's within us, I believe. Why would they make us feel like that, if our government is corrupt then there's no problem with people of other countries, if they have good rules of law then our countries should adopt it.

> I think a company, instead of outsourcing, should employ people directly from their country, it will save on costs for the parent country and it will also benefit the individual working for them

> And it will also increase the employee retention rate –

> as if you pay me well for doing remote work for you, I will definitely not denigrate you

> How do you feel about the call centre industry?

> 20.50 PKT

Pretty much the same as every other low-paid industry in this neoliberal dystopia... disgusted and saddened

15.51 GMT

> What can we do to improve it? It's all the same everywhere in the world.

> 20.51 PKT

It is indeed, but many people are so brainwashed here in the UK from ignorance and fear! I don't know 😮 I'm currently in despair ... I stand in solidarity with you guys.

15.52 GMT

> Thanks for being with us.
>
> 20.53 PKT

Do you guys have to work to call turnaround targets?

15.53 GMT

> Yeah – we have certain KPI's to meet,
>
> like chatting with a specific number of clients, the chat should not go longer than three minutes, proper greetings, proper closing remarks and many more.
>
> 20.54 PKT

Yeah I kinda thought so – my company have overseas call centres and it's obvious the agents are highly scripted ... and on a tight turnaround.

Do you find the job stressful?

15.55 GMT

> This is among the world's toughest jobs after air traffic control and it has a lot of stress attached to it, as well –
>
> we feel exhausted, we literally feel pain in our brains
>
> 20.55 PKT

Can you tell me more?

15.56 GMT

> After the shifts we need around 30/40 minutes to get back to normal life.
>
> 20.56 PKT

What specifically makes the job so hard, do you think?

15.57 GMT

> Talking to so many customers at the same time makes it difficult, and ensuring 100 per cent quality assurance along with customer satisfaction is really a difficult thing to do
>
> 20.58 PKT

...

> Thank you so much for sharing your experience with us. I wanted to ask if you receive any kind of support for the abuse you receive from callers? Apart from the training?
>
> 16.01 GMT

>> Well! we get fired if we do something bad with a customer even if he is abusive.
>>
>> 21.02 PKT

> So you don't receive any kind of support, for example, after a particularly bad experience?
>
> 16.04 GMT

>> If it was our fault, like abusing a customer back, then a big No
>>
>> If it was a customer's fault and we retaliated a bit, even then we get a warning letter
>>
>> 21.04 PKT

> That's awful, to hear that your wellbeing is not even supported. I have worked in call centres before, which was awful enough. But UK workers usually receive at least some backup. The dynamic for Pakistan workers is obviously different, and I can't begin to imagine the emotional strain in your position.
>
> 16.05 GMT

>> It's painful but at the end of the day it's our job and we need to do it with honesty and keep looking for something extra for ourselves.
>>
>> 21.06 PKT

> Of course, that is the best that you can do. I am so sorry for the conditions we have caused.
>
> Are most calls about complaints? If so, how do you cope with that? How do you keep the energy level high after draining calls?
>
> 16.07 GMT

>> ...

> We divide calls in 3 groups. Information, Service requests and Complaints, and we receive most calls about information, and yes, if there is some known issue with the service then the complaint calls ratio gets high.
>
> We used to do same practice before our shift for 5 to 10 minutes
>
> 21.09 PKT

Makes sense, to keep the energy high and get things out. Did you ever get "mad" with a customer and respond firmly?

16.10 GMT

> It happens, as we are all human beings and I have faced such incidents many times in my career, but we are not allowed to be rude to customers, we transfer the call to our supervisor and then he handles the customer accordingly.
>
> If I become rude, I can lose my job.
>
> we deal with mixed emotions everyday
>
> angry, happy, obnoxious, abusive, sarcastic, taunting, appreciative, well behaved,
>
> a good call keeps us motivated for next few hours
>
> and 1 bad call can ruin the day easily
>
> but now we are trained enough to not to take such things at our heart
>
> 21.11 PKT

I have had to make complaints to call centres before (to the bank or medical matters, for instance) and I always feel bad that my frustration comes out with the person on the end of the phone, who really has nothing to do with the issue!

16.12 GMT

...

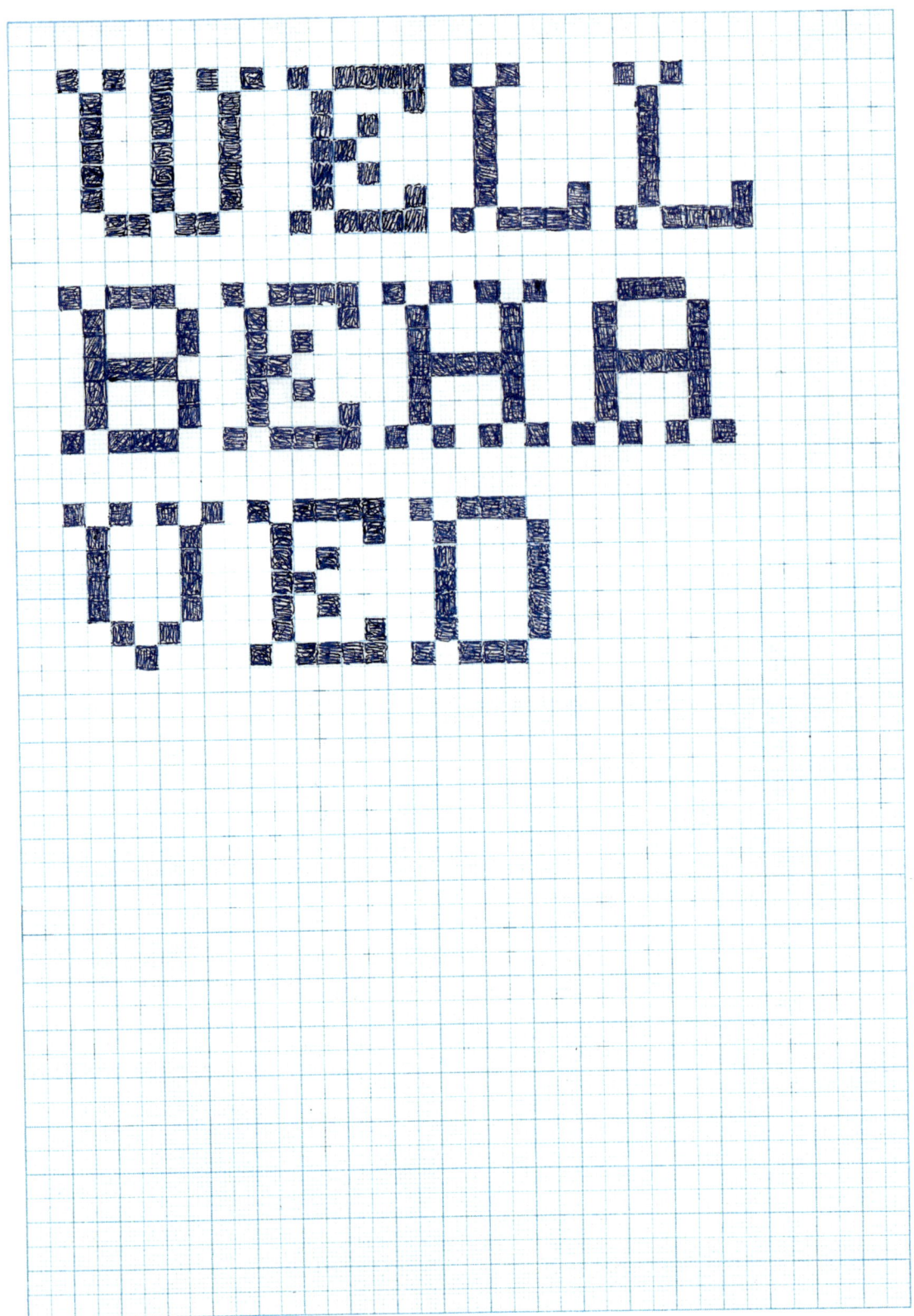

31   *Well Behaved* (drawing), 2022,
blue pen on graph paper, 210mm x 297mm

32   *Well Behaved* (framed), 2022, blue pen on graph paper
and pink post it on a file folder. 660cm x 491cm x 5cm

> We feel very bad about it and we try to ensure that you don't call for the same reason again as if you call within 48 hours for the same reason then we face a pay cut due to non-provision of "first contact resolution" – if you are in pain then we get the pain too.
>
> And secondly, we are hired by companies to listen to customers, their abuse, their scolding and all the related stuff.
>
> 21.15 PKT

It sounds tricky to deal with.

I am a bit horrified that you might face a pay cut because of a complaint that is unresolved in 48 hours!

It's not much time.

Also, I was checking on the website: there is a big gap in the time zone between the UK and the USA – do you have to work night shifts? And do you get a better salary if you do so?

16.16 GMT

> If i opt for a USA-based project, i.e. a selling-based project, then I work night shifts; on the other hand, if I work on a UK-based project requiring services only then it's a rotational shift
>
> 21.16 PKT

OK, OK.

16.17 GMT

> Is there anything you would like people to know about more about (about the job)?
>
> 21.17 PKT

First, treat them as you want to be treated, they can scold you but you can't scold them, do not spoil their mood, as this affects their jobs

...

fig. 33,34,35   106,107

> trust me, we are paid very little and on the other hand with this low salary when we listen to an abusive customer, we sometimes want to quit the job right away.
>
> 16.17 GMT

The low salary and annoying behaviour from customers and bosses are the reasons for the high turnover of employees working at call centres.

20.18 PKT

> Thank you for being open and sharing your experience.
>
> It's interesting to know the other side of the chat / call centre –
>
> We can get quite stressed in our lives, and especially when it comes to the point that we need to get in touch with customer services we forget we are talking to people having to do this all day with a bunch of stressed people.
>
> 16.20 GMT

You are welcome! And yes! You are absolutely right but we cannot train the whole of society to talk so that's why people in call centres get such training to listen to scolding and abuse and keep calm.

20.22 PKT

> Are you enjoying being part of this project?
>
> 16.22 GMT

This is something very exceptional. At least we're getting a chance to speak our hearts out

While launching a complaint, deep inside we are also praying that your issue gets resolved in time and you don't call again.

20.24 PKT

> Yes. I can imagine.
>
> 16.24 GMT

Islamabad, Pakistan   15:48:43
London, United Kingdom 11:48:43

33	*Untitled (perfect lovers) 1/2*, 2022, clock, 300mm x 300mm
34	*Website (PKT-GMT time zone)*, 2022, How May I Serve You?, screenshot.
35	*Untitled (perfect lovers) 2/2*, 2022, clock, 300mm x 300mm

> i wanted to play my role, in letting people know that how call center people are spending their lives behind the phone, do they get hurt like normal people?, they do sacrifice their own social life to facilitate them, different shifts and many other things that we do. People should know how we are feel so that the industry get some sort of respect
>
> 20.26 PKT

Agreed. It's an excellent idea and a great platform for some honest conversation.

16.26 GMT

> People don't know how we feel at the other end of the phone, and this project will definitely add value at the agents' end, and this will also give an understanding to customers
>
> 20.27 PKT

Yes, the transparency is really useful for everyone concerned.

16.28 GMT

> True!
>
> I am also amazed to find out that many people didn't know very common things about our industry and it is great to share knowledge with everyone
>
> 20.28 PKT

Exactly. I don't know much about your industry. In just a few minutes I have learnt something about the system that affects both you and me.

Thank you for chatting to me. I now need to go and prepare dinner for the family. It was good to 'meet' you here.

16.29 GMT

> Thank you for being part of this project. it was really nice talking to you.
>
> 20.30 PKT

And you too :-)
16.31 GMT

> Have a nice weekend!
>
> 20.31 PKT

Thanks! You as well.
16.32 GMT

How May I Serve You?: Witness to action
Dr. R.M. Sánchez-Camus

What happens when we bear witness? This is the first step in active participation and responsibility. Bearing witness forces us beyond voyeurism into shared responsibility and complicity. What we do next with this information always remains the challenge for the audiences, who often are firefighting a number of social injustices across various causes.

José García Oliva's practice is part of an important lineage of visual arts that uncovers hidden social narratives, allowing us to shift our interpersonal relationships towards restorative justice and social equity.

This project is an empathetic response tool designed to stimulate and inspire the audience member. The live performance space also moves beyond mimesis to be a living archive of a hidden subject. Malik Ayaz and Saadia Abbasi want "the world to know how people are spending their lives behind the screen. People don't know and often yell at us, they are calling because they have issues which I can relate to, but this doesn't give them the right to scold us or rudely talk to us and spoil our day."

But why an art project? Malik put it best when he described art as "something connected to emotions that gives you a message to take away." This project, for him, was a gate to show what they are not allowed to reveal at work – their emotions.

Just bearing witness and having their stories told is the beginning of an act of emancipation. According to Malik, "no one has ever asked for our perspective before. We were stunned that someone was doing something for us, and I hoped it could create an impact". Armed with this knowledge, we now ask audiences to share this conversation with others and do any action possible to participate in solution-building for a more equitable service world.

José García Oliva

is a Venezuelan artist based in London. His work explores the clash between diasporic identity, migrant labour, and cultural heritage. These collisions are explored through materials, everyday objects, and performative actions that emerge differently from each research project. Oliva's multidisciplinary practice is driven by collaborative processes and aims to react to and expose sociopolitical oppression through participatory performances or public interventions. The result of his work is often the enactment of these social exchanges and provocations shaped by the commons and site specificity. Oliva graduated from the Royal College of Art, London, in 2020 and completed her Bachelor of Fine Arts in Madrid with a mobility grant from the Ministry of Education. Oliva currently leads the Visual Communication postgraduate course at Ravensbourne University and is an associate lecturer at Kingston School of Art.

References

Bain, Peter and Taylor, Phil (2000), *'Entrapped by the "electronic panopticon"? Worker resistance in the call centre'*, New Technology, Work and Employment, 15:1, pp. 2–18, https://doi.org/10.1111/1468-005X.00061. Accessed 24 March 2021.

Bruguera, Tania (2011), *Introduction on Useful Art*, New York: Immigrant Movement International, https://www.taniabruguera.com/cms/528-0-Introduction+on+Useful+Art.htm. Accessed 1 August 2020.

Checchia, Viviana (2017), *Forms of Action*, Glasgow: CCA.

King, Martin Luther (2018), *Letter from Birmingham Jail*, London: Penguin Random House.

Kors, Joshua (2012), 'Alien at the office', ASX, 6 February, https://americansuburbx.com/2012/02/lars-tunbjork-alien-at-the-office-2004.html. Accessed June 2020.

Marchart, Oliver (2019), *Conflictual Aesthetics: Artistic Activism and the Public Sphere*, Berlin: Sternberg Press.

Orwell, George ([1949] 2008), *Nineteen Eighty-Four*, London: Penguin.

Thompson, Nato (2012), *Living as Form: Socially Engaged Art from 1991–2011*, New York: Creative Time Books.

Thank you all for your kind support. Without you, this project would not have been possible.

Adela Blanco, Aditya Ganged, Adrian Shaughnessy, Aesha Haider, Alberte Lauridsen, Arthur Schulz, Ascensión Hernandez, Asma, Bakhtawer Haider, Betty Brunfaut, Cathy Johns, Celestine, Chiara Piccirillo, Christopher, Christopher Flagg, Clara Dahan, Colette Brunfaut, Dan Aneiros, Daniel Baez, Dan Nicolae Barzu, David Grynberg, David Pichardo, Emilie Cleeremans, Emily Wells, Eugenia Del Rosario, Fabio Castro, Fátima Oliva Pérez, Gerard Eykhoff, Hannah Rozenberg, Heliodora Pérez Martín, Henry Schwartz, Jacqueline Duret Bielen, James Roadnight, Jamie Jenkinson, Jasper Jeurissen, Jeanne Brunfaut, João Villas, Joshua W. Davies, Juliette Duret, Laura Gordon, Lauren Velvick, Lola Boom, Lydie Nesvadba, Madeleine Kessler, Malik Ayaz, Magda Tritto, Margherita Sabbioneda, Marianna Helena Janowicz, Max Ryan, Michael Serritella, Mike Cassella, Nida Akram, Omer Alraee, Oriana García, Paul Wilson, Pedro José García, Pedro Trino García, R.M. Sánchez-Camus, Sadia Abbasi, Sebastian Van Velzen, Shahzad Haider, Sherry, Siohely García, Sukhdev Sandhu, Thandi Loewenson, Thierry Brunfaut, Tiny Finn, Kristina Chan, Vicky Evans, Victoria Molenkamp, Victoria Petelin and Zhenming Kwan.

A thousand thanks

Edited and Designed
by José García Oliva

Live-chat
Malik Ayaz & Saadia Abbasi

Proof-reading by
Cathy Johns

Printed and bound
by Plain.tiff Press

Typeface
IBM plex

Published by Sold Out Publishing
www.sold-out.net
info@sold-out.net

ISBN978-1-914180-05-7

© Copyright 2023
José García Oliva
and Sold Out Publishing
All rights reserved.

We Use English Names 2/2, 2021,
Acrylic on wood, various sizes.